# Saving the
# World
# From Self

## Or Should I Say
## Selfishness

# Saving the World From Self

## Or Should I Say Selfishness

Phillip Regman

Reflections on the Past

*First Edition*

**Reflections on the Past**

A division of
www.HiddenBrookPress.com
writers@HiddenBrookPress.com

Saving the World From Self: Or Should I Say Selfishness
by Phillip Regman

Cover Design – Richard M. Grove
Layout and Design – Richard M. Grove
Front cover art – Armando Alleyne
Back cover art – Mary Ann Kikerpill

Typeset in Garamond
Printed and bound in UAS

Library and Archives Canada Cataloguing in Publication

Regman, Phillip, 1958-
  Saving the world from self : or should I say selfishness /
Phillip Regman.

Poems.

ISBN 978-1-897475-65-2

  I. Title.

PS3618.E478S29 2010          811'.6          C2010-907668-0

Dedicated to:

Becky Catlett—typist,

friends in the writing lab at C.O.S

Institutions, Agencies, Organizations,

People that are committed not only to the service of others

but to the responsible service to others

and to the Glory of God.

A Very Special Thanks to those friends

that have made this book a possible event.

# Table of Contents

# Foreword

*Saving the World From Self: Or Should I Say Selfishness* is often dubbed the what if it were me book. It is a sympathetic view of the effects of selfishness as well as a progressive, interactive invitation to engage support, resolve and understanding.

I heard it said, "There's nothing new under new under the sun", "Do unto others as self", "Love your neighbor as your self", Saving the world from self or should I say selfishness is a fresh take on a concept that has probably been around since forever.

Saving the world from self or should I say selfishness deals with time honored traditional concepts like loneliness, longing, gratitude, abandonment and proposes each one does make a difference to each others living condition- how significant maybe very well up to you. Ultimately we can further improve the living conditions for everyone-everywhere.

The world isn't really that big of a place and God is bigger than all of us.

Let us, by our interactions influence to each other what is good support.

Don't judge the messengers' choice of words or presentation but rather enjoy the delivery of the concept. Sharing, caring, living, dying all the stuff in between like community, support, growth, continued growth understanding and applied continued growth. Saving the world from self or should I say selfishness explores relationships, friendships, making love, sex, communication, consideration, and the stories are not to be missed nor their points of interest ignored.

Because everyone is unique Saving the world from self can take on new meanings and or different understandings for as many people who read the book. No wonder its often dubbed the *what if it were me book.*

# Midnight Christmas Eve
# At
# Your House

Old country road
By the light of the moon, I saw "Your House". (church)
Smoke from the chimney where we stayed,
Where we shared ourselves family for the holiday.

Old country road
By the light of the moon, I saw "Your House"
Where you welcomed us strangers in
Regardless of race, color, creed, or class,
And we shared ourselves family for the holiday.

In the distance the pine trees combed the night sky
In shades of silver, they towered the night endless
With feelings of warmth and special holiday thanks.

In the distance the subtle waters continuing flow
Could be heard. Almost without effort,
Soothing and Enduring,
The sound of the waters continuous flow generated
A heightened sense of purpose and peace
Which made me feel blessed in its acknowledgement.

Old country road
By the light of the moon,
I was moved, by the night's stillness.
The stillness of winter's foliage
And the onset frost of coming snow.
I was moved by the strength of unity
And the greater force of good will,

Toward all, in "Your House",
—Where you welcomed even us strangers in
And allowed us to be moved
By the power of "Your House",
To change even the very course of our lives,
As we shared ourselves family
With others for the holiday.

Old country road
My face expressed an overwhelming awe.
My cheeks were wet from tears
That flowed from my eyes: full.
My tears bared proof to the truth
That the beauty of what I saw,
Heard, tasted, touched and felt,
Must directly connect to the presence of God
And peace of home in my heart.

May you too experience what encompasses
With all your senses, God's glory
And may you share it with others better than I,
For the glory of God. Amen.

# Faith Proceeds All

When we get together
We let go of I
And I becomes we are
And what's mine becomes ours
Our time together is fun in fellowship
We share, we talk, we listen—we grow
Without drink or drug
We find the courage that is already there
To put into action what we already know
—God is good!

Whenever we get together
I become you
You become we are growing in fellowship

Come one come all
Come high or low in the Lord
Come who are lonely
Come who are afflicted, restricted,
Ridiculed (good kids suffer too when they just say no)
Come rich, come poor
Come Bi-polar, energized, depressed and hyper-active
Come one, come all
Come high or low in the Lord

Because God's love equals us all
We welcome the strangers,
The sinners the saints even old men
That wear funny hats and polka dot shoes
Women that wear woolen mittens and polka-dot
Rouge because we remember
They become us when I become you

# Liquid Tones of Silence

Liquid Tones of Silence
Uncap and distribute
The melancholy pouring its way through

Liquid Tones of Silence
Echo beneath fathom waves of sorrow
Torment tomorrow's slave.

Liquid Tones of Silence
Uncap and distribute this prop we use
Abusing cycle
Melancholy over life—we choose grief to reclaim

Liquid Tones of Silence
Hoist fun the sails! Fly high the masses!
But remember, seagulls can follow
To pick clean till the bones are bare and sorrow.

# The Value of Honesty

I sat on the edge of the water
I took in its flow
I became one with the flow
And its dimples made by the sun's reflection
On the water's remains
Easing by ever so steady—with a smile

I took in the sound of the waterfall

Like the steady flow of soothing
Bath water running in a tub
It felt like I'm about to get in and be calmed,
Relaxed, released,
And cleansed from the inside out—
Ready to restart whole,anew
Fresh—clean, more correct.
Is this poem about confession
Talking to a parent, friend, or relative
Or simply the value of honesty?

# Relationships

Nothing is perfect
But if you see what you like
It can be perfected to your liking-

Nothing is ever complete
Unless it is made whole first
But yet and still
There's no guarantee
For you
For me / only that the world is…
Full of relationships.

# Point of Intersection

If: A line is a series of dots
Then: How many angles to an angle?


If: Your answer is 360
It might be close if we were going round inside a circle
If: your answer to: How many angles to an angle
Depends on how many people are present or
The study of images is infinite or
The study of television is the greatest study of images
Then: What about the movies
Are we inside generations of stereotypes
Going round and round?

# Assuming Roles

*In assuming roles, it isn't difficult*
*To see how much fun growing can be...*

"You do you"
It's okay because you can hold your own doing you
And I think it's cool but I think if we ever got together
Who would hold their own
Who would play the fool

"You do you"
It's what I think you're doing anyway,
when you're not here
Despite what you show me,
I wonder if we ever got together
What would I see in you or you in me
Except for this reality of friendship
No matter how the screw turns
 in a bending force of a weak moment.

"You do you"
Can you hear me like I listen to you.
I'm confused about the love I feel for you
And this love, at this time
Is governed by the laws of friendship
Me nearer and you nearer too
Growing from the trust of our communication
Don't want to complicate the matter by rushing things.

"You do you"
And you're a strong willed doing you
With a sense of integrity I feel to trust
And with every needing moment,
I choose to make you feel
every bit of special that I feel for you

And my treatment for this?
You would think it was cruel if I were you and you were me

"You do you"
It's okay 'cause you can hold your own doing you too
But if we ever got together
If you make a point, then let me make mine.
Need to hear what I need to say
So we can move forward and not stuck on
Padding the point, Run- on manipulations or fribble.

"You do you"
If I proceed myself offensively dominate
With fatherly urgencies for clarification and well being

It's how I feel toward you
I feel it's my duty, duty, duty
To show you love the only way I know how
I must and I will toward myself be true to me, you, and duty

*In assuming roles, you are responding verbally*
*what you believe to be the real feelings of another out loud,*
*exactly how you believe they would*
*if they could if you were them and they were you.*
*In assuming roles, it isn't difficult to see*
*how much fun growing can be for you and me.*

# That He Was...
# Just as Smart as You

There was a friend of mine,
His name was Clyde.
Some say he was dumb: others dumb and retarded
But the truth was...
That he was just as smart as you.

We spoke of religion
With a hint of vision,
Economics, Reganomics,
Philosophical opinions and do.
Some say he was a social misfit: others retarded.
But the truth was...
That he was just as smart as you

He was quite versatile.
He associated with all people—"the good,"
"the bad," he also knew.
Real class is not snobbery or better than
And can go anywhere on any level.
The truth was...this is what helped make Clyde
Just as smart as you.

# Master's Rights

He mounts her with all the energy of hate,
Anger and frustration
Compounded by his hard day's work
Or maybe due to his drinking,
He burdens her receptive to his releases.
With the strength of a savage superman
He compounds her receptive to his releases.
He vents and confuses his hate,
Anger and frustration with making love,
Making good strong hard love
He penetrates her
I could only imagine
With the force of a horse backing a cow
And in her MEOW she confuses her ripped torn flesh
With making love.

He beats her like a man fighting in the ring for money.
He breaks her and keeps her broken
Much like a bully catching an insect
And detaching its wings or legs for fun
And she confuses this,
She confuses her pain with love's bliss.

He strong wills her into submissiveness
Until even his very thought
(which she must anticipate in advance and quickly)
Is carried out

In her slavery,
He delights her low self-esteem
That confuses partnership with master's rights.
In her slavery,
He continues to reduce her
And in the relation she is rendered helpless.

In her slavery,
In her abduction from herself
In what seems to be a circle of torment
Now with a broken jaw, she pretends to be happy,
Even secure
Knowing her only peace is Master's rights
And my tears flow
From her crying over denying
And confusing Master's rights with love.

# Mattie's Kid

She looked at me with a twist of lemon
That made me stand on edge.
Uneasy, like just before
having to take castor oil in the morning.

Knowing how important it was
To make a good impression
Even as a kid,
But still secretly trying to decide would I like her
Quickly trying to analyze was she a nice lady
And would I like her now or later
My mother left the room as I said,
"Pleased to meet you ma'am,"
(She was a friend of my mother's.)

When she looked toward me her eyes gave me
An attitude that said,
 "So this is Mattie's kid"
She spoke past me to the other adults in the room
As if I didn't matter, As if I wasn't there
As if I could not possibly have feelings,
Being a kid back then
Nor did it seem possible to me that she seemed to care.
I believe
Kids should be seen and heard all the time.

# On This Earth

On this Earth—in this world,
I make my home.

No time like the present
No present like time
Expression—responses
Aggressions and defensives.
I become—we are,
We are great to be alive and well
On this Earth—in this world,
I make my home.
In this space I become—we are
And because we are one
Then Happy my Birthday to you.

# Consideration

If there is a slam here, it's just for those trifling kids
Whose good parents work hard.
Busy, putting food on the table
And paying bills to bother with the infantile attention seeking,
Self-absorbing, self-centered,
Ungrateful selfishness of I, and always me: trifling kids.

Get busy
Considering being responsible
Consider contributing to the household or team
(at least with good grades if you're in school)

If there is a slam here,
It's for those trifling kids
Whose constant fuss and bickering is really a cry for help
But because of their own poor attitude about themselves,
Goes unnoticed
And deprives them of the very help they cry for
Dissatisfied about everything,
Expecting everything to be given
Even weekly allowance for chores half-done,
Or not done at all

Get busy considering being useful to the world round you
Who wants a useless chronic complainer
Sponging through life's good times
Off of friends and family anyway?

If there is slam here,
It's for those same kids that grow up or rather, get older
That have conditioned themselves to think the world owes them
And maybe, their sexy bodies will be all they ever need
One relationship after another and another and another

Never learning consideration,
Responsibility or contributing
Cause maybe,
They never learned gratitude or consideration first.

# In the World, Under the Skin

In the world, under the skin
Like inside where tongues and gums collide or
Where tongues hide under the word mountainside.
There's practical reality, magic
Or unlimited treasure which can be found
Accessed by many names,
Just know this is how it can be done with skill
And there are many responsibilities for doing it right.

In the World, Under the Skin
Like where Mack the knife lives comfortably.
It's almost insane to think the body as a machine of pressure.
Directed by the very words we use, we choose.
This underlining reality may be hard to comprehend at first.
No road maps to follow. Rules vary except for one.
Unto others as self is safe.
Cause what goes round today could come back tomorrow.

In the World, Under the Skin
Like time, Like Prayer, Usually an adult thing,
A mother's gift if you wish or
Singer or actor's craft if you had to put a lid on a secret,
And wing it.

Gas has pressure.
Pressure creates energy.
Words channel the energy into becoming clear,
Focused and real.
Breathe deep what can't be told but effects can be measured.
To the degree of what's practical reality
Or magic or unlimited treasure.

*Unmetered guess (ie)*
*Dressers can't pretend to mend a sin again.*

Is a crazy line that rhymes to a timely smile
Let's proceed.
Let's find the smile that's yours
Let's find the smile that opens doors.

In the beginning was the idea,
And will turned into words, brought it forth.
The idea here is words are powerful.
Words communicate ideas, ideas shape our lives
From our lips words shape many things
If: we can read and write mathematics
Then: surely we can use words to shape unto our lips a smile
Let's find the smile that's yours
Let's find the smile that opens doors.
*One sided clowns cannot be ignored*
*Nor are igloos for swimming.*
Is a crazy line that rhymes to a timely smile.
Pomegranates! You troubadours. Go today Go!

# I

If: A mother knew a son such as me,
As me and mine,
Then: None

# II

With your heart alive, in my heart,
Is then death really a great illusion?

# III

If attitudes can be healed or realigned
Through conversation,
Then, let's talk, let's talk, let's talk.

# IV

We're all sinners,
But we don't have to act like it
—all the time.

# V

Over
Night:
Came tomorrow.

# VI

"It seemed like a waste of time living
If you were a slave woman
Married to a husband that beat you too."

# VII

Even grapes,
Fermented
Can still become good wine.

# An Autumn's Overview

Everytime we meet,
There is an unbalanced serenity
That lean our way.
These priceless and angelic forms
Dispense without lack of concernment or conservativeness
Only the enjoyment of our way.
Like Mr. Magoo and Felix the Cat,
These angelic forms unleashed themselves savage
Toward our release and motivation.
We breathe to the sounds of quick wit, fast-thinking
Rising to the heights of hope for a better tomorrow
Over time, the delivery changes,
Some more clever than others.
Overcoming the odds makes change
A recovering process sometimes.
Over, and over.
But the story must be told, even as adults
There's hope for a better tomorrow
And good overcomes evil traditionally.

I stand at the roof's edge,
The night is full of glow.
I stand at the world's edge,
Overwhelmed by the lights
Above, beyond, and below.
We synchronized submissions
Through undertones of blue-gray,
Gray, black, and white together.
In autumn and overview

Of this patios serenity to follow.

The winding road to end is here
Because it was twice there
Which points back to every time we meet
There is a sunrise to a sunset
And the promise of twilight
Beyond there rising for you and me.

# When I Write

I laugh when I write,
I sing when I write,
To compose my thoughts to the point of you

I shout when I write,
Cry when I write,
To compose my every effort
Into getting just that much closer

I release honesty from the heart
In hope that you will respond favorably
Toward my intentions or attentions

I reason into a resolve when I write,
To understand to the very core of why.
I share myself when I write,
Linking myself into your situations
And becoming your situation to find a resolve.
*Growing can still be fun.*

I speak when I write,
And it is those thoughts that connect
With your thoughts
To delegate a sense of composure,
Excellence, and fair play
And for this, God is good!

# We Stay the Course

*In Memory of 9/11*

Bonnie goes off to work one day.
She kisses her kids off to school,
Pretty much the same way,
Not knowing this day would be her last.
Little David cries, as every night Mommy dies,
Mommy dies in his dreams.
"Who's going to take care of us?"
He asks: his troubled mind had this new task.
Thinking of the future, for him and his sister too
"Will Grandma come soon or will it be you?"

Three weeks later, in the time of early dawn,
The sky was still cloudy
The moon was not over though sunrise was gone.
Pale white, misty thick paste colors you could taste
Were the colors that went by. Peace,
Hope, and strength united were holding a close tie.

The Son seems to have disappeared,
But I know it's clear to me,
Simply by the light of day,
The comfort in a tone
That He is here.
So the promise of tomorrow
And things to come will be – will be.
And so every night these three weeks that have gone by,
I ask the Lord to bless and protect
All the little Davids who lie in their beds and cry
Of Mommy—of Bonnie.

My Bonnie I remember you by the rail,
By the water, by the lighthouse in the dark.
My Bonnie who lies somewhere
Underneath the skyline in the City of New York.
As every night Bonnie dies,
Out loud Mommy dies,
Completing Little David's dream.
Flagrant fumes of despair rise
Amid the crowds worldwide—
They mourn the loss of those gathered round.
We want to frown
But we cry to God:
We cry to God to stay the course.

To stay the course without panic yet,
Anger and sorrow holding true our liberty's intact,
Allowing forever better days to come,
We stay the course
We stay the course.

# People and People

Mirror, Mirror on the wall, let's talk about what we see
In this survival mission we have before us as life.

If: There's order to the universe
Then: My given, A study of the "earth worm"
In a "water surrounding."
If: You put an earth worm onto a "water" surrounding
To live and had it guarded by "patrolling fish troops"
And, a "turtle" to supervise supremely,
And if: "The earth worm" be the "black man,"
And "the turtle" be "the government,"
Then: What would the study of "this study"
Of the "earth worm" be?

For you, for me, first believe the truth.
I learned every "white" person isn't your enemy
And every "black" person isn't your brother.
People are people
We are a species called human
We collect and retain issues. Sometimes we act on them.
It is our continuing effort,
To achieve and maintain what is humane.

# Friday:
# Under Urban City Night Sky

Two rode together.
They stood side by side.
One was boredom; one was pride.
Under Urban City Night Sky.

People going,
Traffic moving
Forms its own lullaby.
Trees on the avenue
Spread at attention
Bicycle flags
Wave a shiny salute speeding by.
On Friday nights,
Chinese restaurants are in command.

Stunning lampposts
Peek above the crowds.
People groovin'
Traffic movin'
Forming their own lullaby.

Night after night
The busses stop.
The screeching halt on the brakes
At the same spots.
Brother, who got dimes?
People prancin'

Despair entwines what is
Their frilly follies.
Full-mooned warm air
Under Urban City Night Sky

Moving like they
Really have somewhere to go.
Kids on the avenue
Playin' in droves,
And only who knows
Who has the dimes?

Beautiful afternoon
Turns into live, misty funk

Under Urban City Night Sky

Don't know why
Night makes the boredom rise
Under Urban City Night Sky

Sounds of laughter and frolic
Like ovations of applause
Overwhelm curious persuasion
That I am, upon occasion,
Kids having fun.
Brother, who got the dimes?
Want to mask
Want to medicate the boredom
The sorry me,

The dull me, alone and feeling lonely me
Under Urban City Night Sky

# Longitude and Latitude
# (Lovers on the Line)

Longitude and latitude lovers on the line we call them
So close they are when they come together
Like a well matched couple grateful to have found each other.
Their eloquent charms-there (on family Saturday)
They're a lot of fun- there (on family Saturday)
We all are too (a lot of fun on family Saturday)
Two pair playing cards to music, to compete,
Win or draw—there
And just for the sake of argument
We're not happy unless we have one
(*A family Saturday argument*)
I still say fish- never fishes.

Because crossing a bridge saves time,
I was inspired by a compelling mood
To urgently conclude balance.
When longitude and latitude meet—
At my house on what we dub family Saturday.
Neutral ground becomes mutual ground
Love struck and willful ground,
Truce, fight, win or stare ground becomes
Grounds for committing to open
And continue development.

Longitude latitude (lovers on the line) we call them
In a special place cause we see how they complete each other
But if only they could, if only they would
Not having to impose our will for
Them to match couple or bond
Cause they already do
Cause they are already there.

Hoping that one day,

They will bond to realize the potential
Of their bonding as a pair
Instead of crossing at the meet or intersecting in the heat.

Can longitude and latitude lines really ever meet and
Travel together toward one direction?
I guess only in a love poem
If only they could,
If only they would see how easily they complete each other.
If this sounds like a silly poem
About geography and hypothetical lines
On some navigational chart,
It is not.
Cause we love them
We see them peeking to their very best
When they come together.

Maybe, longitude and latitude are two lines or lovers
That must never travel toward one direction together.
But only connect to grounds for committing
To open and continued development.

Because each holds their own communicating so well
And so well together
No one knows how the end will go
Only the rest is that: true love must follow
True love will allow… completion
So,
There.

# Keja Tyin

Penny- red- Broadway,
Abner-Elfin-McClaine.
Because of "Bewitched," and "Sleeping Beauty"
Surely where ever I am-Keja will always tie in...

Keja Tyin Regman girl,
Sneaking with her brother, Phil
Goodies of the pantry,
Goodies like popcorn, potato chips,
Cookies, cakes and candy.
As we both got spankings later during the day,
Hoping to blame each other
We'd yell each other's names
And till this day, I still say
Keja Tyin was to blame.

Early to bed-sometimes we'd rise at five
Sneaking into the living room,
"Davey and Goliah" was the first 'toon on.
We liked "Deputy Dog," "Mighty Mouse,"
And "Heckle and Jeckle;"
We liked "Courageous Cat and Minute Mouse."
Like "Top Cat" those 'toons are gone.
Up close to the T.V. set we sat,
Singing to the bouncing ball
And when the song was finished,
Whom do you think we heard

Coming from down the hall?
Clutching her night coat over her sleeping gown,
She marches into the room. Hoping
To appease the angry look on her face. We said,

"Mommy, mommy, we love you!"
But it didn't change a thing.
As we both got spankings later during the day,
Hoping to blame each other,
We'd yell each other's names.
And till this day, I still say,
Keja Tyin was to blame.

Halloween was fun that year Ghosts and Goblins about
I was a junior Batman; Keja was a Linda Good Witch Sprout.
We came home with big loot that night:
Goodies—Two pumpkin gallons full and more

But when the morning came, the candy was gone
Hoping to appease the angry look on her face we said,
"Mommy Mommy, we love you!"
But it didn't change a thing.
As we both got spankings later during the day
Hoping to blame each other
We'd yell each other's names
And till this day I still say
Keja Tyin Regman Girl was to blame.

# VIII

One and one
Doesn't always equal two.
Sometimes they
Make what was part:
Whole.

# IX

If: You had a big argument
With your mother
And till her dying day
Hadn't put it behind you

Then: who really grew up
And who remained the same?
Simply: Who remained "apparent"
Who remained a "child."

# X

At first glance
A tree can seem to be dead
—Until Spring.

# XI

Raw around the edges
Is what a diamond is
In the rough.

# XII

I walk funny,
I talk funny,
I am funny, or so I appear to be
Because many times its easier
To deal with, humor and "funny"
Than the real issue of pain.
Could this be true for you too, sometimes?

# Mate-tum

She was looking for someone to dominate
Why she settled for me (soft-spoken guy that I am)
I guess made me a choice candidate.

She was secure about her weight
She was exclusively demanding.
She was conservative in her conversation;
Her convictions were never bending.
It was that
That drew me back from a position
I might otherwise have favored.

She was charmingly light on her feet. Debutante,
She wore pearls to bed on black satin sheets,
But her opinions were her convictions.
They were never bending.
They did not for any reason waver
If she compromised just once-met me in the middle
She would have been very clever.

She dictates, ultimate-tums"
That are in short, "verba-tums."
Never to meet anyone in the middle,
I realized she would survive the rest of her life
Without man, woman, or "mate-tum."

# Just For Today

*In rehab it was or so the story begins...*
*As I walked into the sun through the meadow*
*And sun beaming on my face, by the lake I saw deer*
*Heads up, buck, doe, and fawn prance noble-like*
*In a kind of splendor-the splendor of family.*

I couldn't help feel drawn near to my own sense of family
And why I was alone
Alone, without family
Christmas without family
New Year's without family
And to whom could a birthday be happy-without family?

What horrendous thing I must have done, that they remember?
—And I did them.
How difficult it is for a mother to see
A monster change in what seems like overnight
In the one she loves and nine months carried
And how difficult it is in the middle of the night
To hear a knock- knocking at the door for money,
And begging for money,
—And needing more—more money

She would tell it if she were here, how difficult it is for
A mother to come home to find her money gone.
To put out of the house and on to the street
One she loves and nine months carried.

Some families make a point
Never to ever, ever, ever, let you forget
Your shameful need
Your shameful deeds for money
It is those same consistent,
Persistant even harassing reminders
That you acknowledge very much as blessings later.

And when I get to thinking about family
Although change effects change
I do have a sense of—just for today.

# All I Knew

Some people are successful
Through learning and higher education
—They're the lucky ones.
All I knew was one and one make two

Some people are successful through inheritance,
Smart business partners or investments.
I took my trust to the Lord, and left it.
It was what I learned how to do.
Because all I ever knew, was one and one make two.

Some people are talented, others just plain lucky.
But all I ever knew was one and one make two.
For me, for you, the truth.

# If You Will

Watching stiff people can make you bored.
And hard.
And dead in a sense.
If you will,
If you will allow it happen to you.
Watching stiff people can make you bored.
And it can make you hard.
And dead in a general sense.
And it can happen to me too.
If you will,
If you will, allow it to happen to you.

# Figures

*His commentaries always started...*

"My son is growing up
Just got his apartment today
I tried to help him raise himself right
—Give him simple equations about life.
And secretly attempt to suggest
How best he can apply, achieve,
and still hold up the light."

*He was a cool, older guy.*
*We liked listening to him deliver*
*his commentaries with enthusiasm.*
*His commentaries always started...*

"My son is growing up
But for right now, he wants to need me in his life.
Figures what us parents be—for you, for me.
Molding kids can be so much fun—
I still remember like yesterday, the silent I told-you-so's
With just a look, this could be done.
And the hurt puppy dog look, and cry on the shoulder.
When there was a problem or something wrong.
It is in those times, you tell your kids you love them.
Without a word being said—and it says so much more.
Like immediate release when you're congested.
Or sudden phone calls in the dead of night,
But everything's alright.
Or simply that, my son is growing up
And still wants to need me in his life."

*He always had a new quote.*
*We didn't always understand right away.*
*Like words from a monologue or a scene from a play.*
*We look forward to seeing him every other Saturday.*

*He talked while the barber cut our hair.*
*He talked while the barber cut his hair.*
*And listened to us—as we and barbers joined in;*
*Always good conversation.*
*He challenged our thinking.*
*We were motivated by the barbers and him.*
*We were young kids then but we felt like young men.*

*His commentaries always started...*
*My son is growing up, but what we didn't know then,*
*Was the older man's son died in birth along with his wife.*
*And that we became "my son" for him.*
*He continued one day on a softer note and said,*
*Should time fly and I'm gone into the long run...*
*Winter is a season.*
*Season is a part of change, change is part of life.*
*All good things come from God.*
*Daily count your blessings.*
*Praise the Lord and continue.*
*If you fall, wisdom to know the difference—*
*Till your journeys end.*
*With every effort, to be of service,*
*To further improve the world's human condition,*
*You will be at the same time, improving your own.*
*To this day I remember him—we remember him,*
*That man in the barbershop—*
*We were kids then but we felt like young men.*

# Volcano In A Box

If I put all the orgasms I ever had in a box,
Would the earth quake?
Would a roar across the continents
Be heard and valleys crumble
Or would the earth expand itself to new horizons—
Maybe to the gates of heaven central?

If I put all the orgasms I ever had in a box,
Would we have to call on the Lord for mercy
And give to the Nile a new meaning for the word flood?
Would Pandora be aroused?
Would a hole be safe
Or would feet run and knees crawl to a safe hiding place?
For you,
For me,
First believe the truth.

## "Wee Little Fly"

"Wee little fly"
On the wall I see you fall.
And you drop from the wall; crawling to me,
Begging me for forgiveness.

"Wee little fly"
Back and forth, round and round,
As I naked myself I do believe you stand still.
To observe the motions of my will.
To the window you go


I see you plain
Then to the corner you go,
Hiding from me and swatter in hand.

"Wee little fly"
Should I come to you with swatter in hand?
Then come to me from your corner hiding from me
So that we may both have peace.

"Wee little fly"
I'm not a violent man
But you have become a mathematical implication
Suggesting angle approaching
Gears for precision to peace.

# Judgments Rendered

We meet for the first time you're quite the looker.
Longing to see really who you are,
I look past your dress and taste in clothes.
I look past how I feel you look to me.
I listen to your speech,
I look past your wisdom or ignorance—
I look past judgments rendered.

We meet for the first time you're quite the looker.
I look past your superficial enclosures,
Past defense and arrogance,
Past some fears, and some pains.
I look past what I feel may be vanity
And ploys to condense with intimidation.
I look past you looking at me,
To see what I feel is your very spirit, sometimes
I pretend doctor, and its "healing time."
Sometimes what I feel I see
Fills me with wonders from God.
Sometimes I don't like what I think I see, or what I feel.
But I always try to be aware of you looking past me.
I try to be aware of what God has done for me.
And acknowledge his glory my judgments rendered.

# 8B Over Wink and Snow

Through clouds of storm
Rage the winds in A flat minor,
Then violin to cello do tenors grow.
The sun's movement—sprays rays through the sky.
Rock and roll does the home of brave thing
—Oh, forecast snow.

By night I do the shuffle walk
To my side-view mirror and window where,
"Four pyramids" guard
"The grave of the mountain witch king."
In the night air they tower bright
Like the flag that seals
My approval in Gramercy Park below.
(*What crazy things we imagine*)
—Oh, forecast snow.

Seven twenty a.m. tormenting whispers at thy host
They pull in waves to drown me,
Pull in droves to distract myself from me.
Grandiosity is flowing here
(*or can't you tell mornings are manic.*)
The sun pierces through blue-gray clouds,
Shining like halos on my window, on my pain
—Oh, forecast snow.

Trying to control me, you seek to console me
—Like I'm going to bend
You feel it's my arrogance that offends you
That defies and intimidates your ability to control me
—It annoys you.
It eats at you because I'm younger and older than you.

*(I guess I'm just another crazy man*
*Whose therapeutic attentions command*
*This very interesting  communication.)*

Past tense,
Future tense come together here
Come together where fame and fortune greet me
—Takes me by surprise and I'm not bitter anymore,
For having waited so long.
*("Now with one foot in the grave and all.")*

Divinity shields surround me.
I think to myself
I'm younger and older than I, than you
Than he, she, it ever was.
—Oh, forecast snow.

How do you squeeze these troubles into my head?
That cast doubts that confine my attentions to 8 Bernstein.
Over suffering, over trauma, terror over cold
—Oh, forecast snow.

My arrogance protrudes my drooping spirits.
My cravings soar—the voices go berserk.
In my depression they try to control me
They try to consume me
They try to consume myself to thee.

Although I suffer my plight
Contentious and self-indulgence paradox
Contentious and compulsive paradox
Me, myself, and I paradox—
I hid my fear of having had lost a marble or two

Behind arrogance turned grandiosity.
Afraid to deal with the shame,
Kept me dealing with the shame
And was the blame for blocking first attempts at help.
*(Isn't denial something?)*

The voices run rampant:
Trying to make up time
For when the medication chased them away.
In my weakness do I indulge them
Or how long will they stay?
—Oh, forecast snow.

Today the nobility of city seek to greet me
To give audience and participation to me
*(Or can't you tell mornings are manic*
*And ego sometimes turns grandiosity?*

My arrogance protrudes my drooping spirits
Depression rising, Rising still
(*I guess you know evening is coming*)
Night is here!
In my depression "the spirits" come to control me.
They come to persuade me to join them
For fun and frolic away, away.
Or they come to get even with me
For having kept them away so long
(*befriending Risperdal and all.*)
They say: they only wanted to share my day,
Learn my way
Hear me pray, help me say.
I choose life.
I choose to come join the world.
I choose 8B over wink.
—Oh, forecast snow.

# Lower East Side Blues

Sunday morning on the lower East Side
Nothing on T.V., it has rained all week
Melancholy morning drinking mood-sleeping mood
Lounging; with nothing to gain nothing to lose.
Such a barrage of excuses, it's hard to pick one
Can I rhyme pain here?
—you know what misery loves

I hear the birds outside in torment
No goodies outside nobody's walking the pavement
Only the early ones knew, come extra early today.
—you know what misery loves and you can't wait to fix it.

My sitter, (my piano)
Distracts me from anxiously waiting your return
As I play- I pay attention to hear the door bell ring
Anxiously waiting to hear that door bell ring
saying you have returned with the goodies.

Sunday morning on the Lower East Side
Sleep-walking across the keys but not wasting time.
Or what sickness calls pride,
I play my piano.
I play by the window to watch for you
"Lower East Side Blues."
To watch from a stranger you meet
From a stranger you greeted that sold you
Death in a package
You couldn't wait to sample the score
You had to sample it before coming to my door
Can I rhyme pain, mourn, sick, or thank God here?

Either way,
—You know what misery loves—lower east side blues.

# XIII

Because you can't always see them,
Doesn't mean they're not there…
Viruses interact and multiply from within
They can reap havoc.
By this same process,
Can we practice more good will in our interactions,
And by our example, further multiply
Peace on earth, from within to change
The outside world into a better place for all?

# XIV

Psst. In America,
No matter what the past
There's always a chance
To salute and be saluted….
If I ever show off
It's to show you that you can too.
Till tomorrow.
I salute you.
Till tomorrow.

## XV

If: the pen is mightier than the sword
Then: there is undeniable power in the word.

## XVI

Are we predisposed to violence
Or is it socially reinforced in our lives?
If: so,
Then: this poem is for you- the image

## XVII

Unto others as self!
Could this still be good news for modern man?

# Slam Too

I start at the top…
Hello, happy to see you.
(Leeway for consideration) I let you speak now
And you start to talk

You continue
And you continue, ignoring my attempts to respond
You continue
Without consideration for me you continue
To refuse to acknowledge
Any attempts from me to speak at all
If: Listening is an active engagement
Then: Could it be that it's more fun taking turns?

# Moving Forward

If: The images from this book
Give you a therapeutic look into a crazy man,
Dishing out love-pure love from a pedestal of poems
Then: You're missing the element of applied self
A fully developed look would intimately
Indicate a picture of sharing inspiration.
To further improve the world for all
And that it continues here with you.
"The value of honesty" has truth.

# There's a Color in the Sky

There's a color in the sky
For every shade of fruit that grows.

There's a color in the sky
For every shade of fruit that grows to know
The seeds they possess will outreach, energize and connect.
There's a color in the sky
For every shade of fruit for every feeling
Or thought these seeds will generate and multiply.
They are in themselves—special selves of God.

Like angels they are sometimes
Their ability to intimately entwine every fabric of our lives
At an instant of a measure—beings of testimony
They are in themselves—special selves of God.

But we sometimes too quickly dismiss them as misfits
We dismiss them because of their dress,
Mannerisms, or appearance
We dismiss them because of sickness
And developmental underlinings
Then we label them, before our dismissal of them
To justify our deed—without guilt.

But sometimes those same seeds,
Maybe because of their exposure to us
Makes them so much brighter,
So much more able to reach out to us and help us
In our connecting to those beliefs we claim.
"Too important" we are "too busy "and "stressed,"
We sometimes too quickly dismiss what we call misfits

And sometimes fail to see;
There's a color in the sky
For which shade of fruit that grows to know better?

# All I Ever Needed Was You

I tried for a long time to say
I love you and me today
But I had trouble staying focused and true
I forgot my simple song was just for you
Every time I tried before
I started thinking instead of feeling the one thing I should
—All I ever needed was you.

I'm not one who can easily hide
My feelings from deep inside
I was sure you would show me how
To let my song travel sincerely to you
—to please you would please me too.
Thinking you ignored me, hurt me somehow
But it was in the hurt tears you brought
That taught me to cry;so i cry outloud.
—All I ever needed was you.

It didn't seem honest at first- for shouting out loud
But once I let go, the release made me feel proud
Getting out the passion bottled in me—that way
Overwhelmed me—that day
—All I ever needed was you.
*Letting the spirit be released in me*
*Letting the spirit have its way with me*
*Starts to come naturally, Lord, naturally.*

# In Thee I Trust

*I close my eyes as I lay down to wake.*
*I pray the Lord my soul to take...*
Remember that prayer as a kid,
On your knees before bed?
Do you really know what you have said?

As a kid, do you remember
Kissing candy from the ground
Kissing it up to God in relief?
Do you really know why you did,
Or what you said?

Ever been in serious trouble
Or threat of danger high?
The very first thing said-
Do you really know why?
And even as a non-believer cries—Oh, Lord!
Could it be what's really being said is in thee I trust,
I place my trust in thee.

# Unto Others as Self
# Or Consideration Goes Both Ways

You never come empty handed...
When you arrive, everyone is glad
That each other has come.
Everyone is anxious to share what they brought with them.

You never come empty handed...
Whether its goodies in a box or bag or bottle or two,
Or excitement about a story of good news,
Or just happy to see you here with us,
Sharing a way- away from the blues.

You never come empty handed...
If the eagle's stretch loses its grip once in awhile,
It's not about what you bring, but what you contribute.
So come as you are
Here all is—one
One is all a team is.
And like team players we're All-stars.
Us enjoying us.
Us engaging us
Us supporting us
In living fun, in living color we are.
(Fuss, fight, win, draw, or stare-there,)
We bear to each other's support.
And like family; or T.V. holiday family dinner—it's special.
We choose to be here.

We choose to be grateful and show it.
We choose to bring something to the table for us.
Us enjoying us, us engaging us.
We are grateful to show friendship,
Is a handful of consideration—that goes both ways.

# On This Rock

On this rock
I build an empire.
I build an empire On This Rock… in Jesus' name.

I combine your situation
With my attitude, a commentary and a point (raw sometimes.)
You give me fame: the fairy tale and happy—ever endings.
I even rhyme sometimes for different reasons.

As long as we both have fun,
As long as we both come—to share us with you—
and you grow to become
We are instead of just I
We are many situations and points to exchange here
Let's grow, Let's share.

Anyway, fair exchange is still no robbery.

On This Rock
I build an empire
I build an empire On This Rock…in Jesus' name.

Sometimes the best way to get
Something you want, something you need
Is simply to ask
And you give me fame the fairy tale
And happy ever endings.
For you, for me

There's no shame in Jesus' name.

# Sharon's Dilemma

"It's quiet," she said.
And we're alone now.
I know what you're feeling and I want to go there.
—More than you know.

She said,
"I give you the power
That gives you the right
To believe it's yours. To overcome
To see through my façade.
And take as yours what I pretend to refuse."

She said,
"And I want you to have, hold, and cherish,
In marriage like you should
What I pretend to refuse
Even when I pretend, it's no use.
And in the strife, I yield it all to you.
Because I made you deserve it."

She said,
"I learned to play the overcome and take game.
From my father and brothers, who took me as a kid.
They taught me only with a struggle,
Could good girls get it—
They could have sex that way."

Please help me to help her see
Love is all we need—no struggle required.
…Sometimes when she sleeps
I hear her clearly, "Stop Daddy!…no!… no!"

# Communication Down Under

I look at you
You look at me.
You grab "it" before the drink.
—It makes me feel sexy
I rise to the occasion
I undress you with all the longing you desire.

Our lips play hot peas and butter
With a twist of lemon, we do that thing
That makes a mouth do that thing
That I like you to do.

I put my mouth to yours
Like you do mine
You tell me it's yours—how I want to hear it
Like how a wife should say it,
You mean for me to hear it

I touch you like you touch me
I feel the wet
I feel the sweat of your reaction
Trying not to look surprised
But happy for the compromise,
You go with the flow
And so, I put my mouth to yours—like you do mine
Cause I love you
I want to please you
And I'm happy you could teach me
How to please you
Like you please me
And to satisfy you with all the longing you desire.
Marriage is a special thing

And made more special with communication down under.

# Cactus Babies

In my heart,
In my heart bleeding for you for me
In my heart bleeding
For babies growing on their own
—Babies alone to grow on their own
Has become a cycle.

How could they make it when mother doesn't know or
Too busy working or just doesn't know
—Babies just can't grow alone—on their own

The song that is sung of this notion:
"A poor little sheep
Without Bo Peep is no security
For little poor babies on their own."
The story that's told was of two kinds of girls
The girls that knew to keep their frame indivisible
Were better able to make it through, while the others,
Went on to create more of themselves
In different versions.

In my heart bleeding for you
Generation's babies of babies

# XVIII

If: Hard ground is made softer
For planting seeds to grow
Then:  Let's open the mind to receive or renew
Grounds for continued development.

# XIX

When you look at kids,
Is it really hard to see
Which parents care and which do not.
Which parents share
And which parents do not.
Which parents are there (providing supervision)
And which parents do not.

Being raised predominately by a single parent,
It can sometimes be hard
For a child to imagine what having
Both parents around is like
Fortunately and unfortunately
My mom cared way more
Than enough for both..

## XX

You don't stop growing as you get older
But who could know this at eight?
I think it's a myth to say;
Too young, too old
Cause the truth is:
Sometime early but never too late.

## XXI

In the wake
Of a solid erection of thought
I took time out
To thank God first

# Love Or Manipulation

They say,
Because of our insecurities as men,
Women have often found it more comfortable
To hold back from their real potential
—For the sake of the relationship
Could this thing they say
Some men do, be a genetic part of me and you?
They say,
If you really love someone,
Do you really expect for them
To shy down from their real potential?
—Purposely limiting themselves subservient
In order for you to feel good,
Comfortable, or secure?
In order to satisfy your quest for dominance?
Or
Is it because women mature quicker than us men
Do they manipulate us,
By our own arrogance and ego,
Into thinking that we should work
While they say
They should stay home?

# Meditation at the Inn

I sat on the mountain
At the edge of serenity
And all its correspondence to me.
A boulder to my right,
A boulder to my left as my security
My security comes from the Lord
With whom all things are possible.

I look over the edge into the valleys
vast fortress of humanity
I praise the Lord for his works
I commune with God's grace
And mountains of life around me
—Better than angels cheering is God's grace
In the environment that surrounds me
Better than nature's healing
Is God's grace that unbinds and heightens me
From just this glance of God's perfection

I sat on the mountain
Compelled by love to love.

# Men Grow Into Men Babies

I watch my hair grow
The length of development
I'm talking about maturity here
I'm talking about you
And me grateful to recognize growth

I watch my hair grow
And I'm given to wonder about
The seasons that change,
That rearrange themselves into our lives
And if we're lucky, we grow.

I think about the moth,
I think about the caterpillar
How they formulate
How they change
Does instinct promote their development to growth
Or do they assume control over their own lives
And choose to let it show?
Does it seem like I'm confusing
Hair with plant, or
Plant with love?
Do they really grow on their own?

What plant can continue to grow in a small pot
Even in a forest—space is needed.
(If: "Plant" is relationship
Then: Who or what can see
A plant growing except for time?)

And at this time…
If this sounds like a silly poem
Going round circles inside
It's about you and me growing
Without demands? Without expectations?
Without obligations or fribble?
Is it possible?
Besides, how can a label change
The direction of a moving heart
And nothing likes to be smothered
Except for pork chops
Or maybe veal for Sunday's dinner.

If: Girls grow into women,—and they do
Then: Men grow into men babies
And we still like to be pampered
—Just not smothered
—Showing us this love, helps us to grow too.

# Safe Journey Into the Long Run

Memories of joy…
My feelings
Abide in a reservoir
Like drink
Like water, but there is no longer taste…

I say "joy" like mother
As if it were a two syllable word
Although we met on many occasions,
I can't say we've been friends lately though
Or friends at all

I do remember my mother
Love, security, joy.
Discipline was the only way of life
What was proper was held in high esteem and taught to me
And I learned it even if it was the hard way

I remember my mother and I
Looking down from her bedroom window
One summer afternoon
When some kid came into the front yard
And plucked her one and only rose
She called him a "little vomit"
And we laughed together for a long time, just her and me.

Also, one day, during a summer afternoon,
While lifting her off the potty
I remember the dead weight
Of her body causing me to fall
We fell together- my mother, me, and the potty

—All over everything
I was hours cleaning up the mess
But finally, when I got her back in bed
And before I secured the diaper,
She urinated
I looked at her in disgust,
And said, "You should be ashamed,"
She looked at me and said,
In a sturdy, but weak old—lady voice,
"I should be ashamed—but I'm not."
And we laughed for days and days behind that one.

My first joy was my mother's love
I remember her coming to pick us up
From Mama Jessie's house (babysitter)
Joy
Opening up gifts on Christmas morning
After Santa had been to our house the night before
Joy
Catching a hint of pride in her face
From something we did, or did not do

Joy

When Keja said, "I love you Mommy."

And I said, as the three of us hugged, "Me too."

Joy

When my Mother, Mr. Leon, Keja and I

Took the bus downtown

To see the first Planet of the Apes

Joy

"If you should leave before us- into the long run

I love you and Keja too

Mother, what ever you decide, it's alright."

*Chow-Chow, Chow-Chew,*

*(the cats) miss the lady, who drops the food on the floor*

*When she eats*

*And wish her a safe passage home or*

*A safe journey into the long run.*

# More Contact

We potted fresh clippings,
Then we labeled the potted plants
Lith positive affirmations
Like patience,
Understanding,
Like self-improvement growing stronger
And take a bigger step today.

*Usually it takes tragedy*
*Or some inspired story*
*Behind a tragedy to get across socially*
*What should be common sense.*
*In addition to medication in the mental health field*
*Shouldn't we also try more contact?*

# People Do Need People

If: Your "family" consists of
The plants in city street windows,
Trees along the avenues,
Fish that you feel sympathy for,
In a tank at a restaurant or a fish store,
Live frogs stuffed like crabs in a basket,
For sale at a China town market,
Or a pet mouse who just has to go everywhere
You go when you leave the house
And a blind cat (Donna Noe Beastrum)
Whose only real comfort was on my shoulder
Especially when leaving the house
(*I don't know who needed whom as a security blanket.*).

If: Your "teachers" consist of
Everything you do
Or know-it-alls or entertainers, scholars and clowns
And friends that time became a witness to—
Or your "Friends" consists of
The sky, the waters,
The sun by day,
The moon by night,
The earth beneath your feet or
Tears of minds, souls, and hearts that cry
Then: May it be a blessing for you
—For me—the truth.
*I've been in and out of my mind so many times*
*That it doesn't make a difference anymore*—
Anyway, you can still get along without people if you had to
—But for how long?
People do need people.

# The Years to Come

One little Indian...taken by business.
Two little Indians couldn't speak English.
Three little Indians didn't know law,
And four met much, much more.

Five little Indians were drugged on maneuvers.
Six little Indian men killed in war.
And one third met much, much more.

Seven little Indians refused to be submissive.
Eight little Indians used as four.
Nine is extinction.
And ten little Indians will probably be the count.
By: the years to come
If: Much more isn't done
If: I said " First believe the truth,"
Would: You laugh?
Then: Where does the buck pass... till the book ends?

# For You, For Me

I walked with my head bowed to the pavement,
Scared to look into your eyes
Scared at what I'd find staring back

I walk with pen in hand
To rescue my caption
My despair, my action
About what I feel
—Might be real
How do I deal with knowing the truth?
How would I know without looking at you?
Afraid to go out—afraid to stay in
Afraid of your approach.
—Will I see you, will you see me?
Will I be happy or disappointed?
And why do guys get so tensed up
Around girls anyway?

I walk with my head bowed to the pavement
Scared to look into your eyes,
Scared at what I'd find staring back
—That you might actually love me too.

# Contact

See the guy on the bench,
Pen and paper subject to the calls of nature
Do you think that time changes nature
Or natures changes in time?

Squirrels seem ambitious.
They gather food, store it for winter.
Are they trying to look "important"
Or have they already learned
Keep working or you will surely starve to death?

See a baby up close.
They breathe in to mimic
The action you deliver.
Is it the same for you and me?
Then can you feel my love?
—Cause it's human nature.

See a Robin build a nest for the future
See the sun set in the sky
Is the day over
Or has another day, really just begun?
And can you tell me why or what is human nature?

# Into Focus

When you come into view
I want to hug you like you hug me too.
But I battle with my insecurities
I battle with events that are past gone
And issues that remain in a crazy brain
That remembers sometimes—somethings
That linger
That point a finger
To lingering resolve—lingering resolve

Like dancing is from the hip
I must get a grip
And compel the force out
Like words come from motive
And travel by way of intention into our hearts
So, I turn this pen on myself
To give clue to therapeutic healing
By way of therapeutic sharing

When you come into view
My fears relieve themselves of me, myself, and I
And in that quiet explosion of a composed moment,
I am entertained cause who I really am is shy.
I am given to hear souls cry
If I can help you hear yours
I wonder if it will help me to hear mine?
And hearts cry too.
And long for success, happiness, and love.

I cry for lost souls
And children scared in the middle of the night

Scared that the boogey-man might come again
Come into their rooms
Into their beds
Into their bodies and cause more hurt
Than you could ever know
And at the craziest of times,
You remember sometimes those things
That linger
That point a finger
To lingering resolve—lingering resolve

I cry for people who find joy in their lives
*(Grateful to God; I don't dare ask where's mine.)*
I cry for happy times and love
*(They tell me all I need is love.)*
I cry for family
*(Of blood and those that time became a witness to.)*

Health, more wealth and love
*(They tell me all I need is love.)*
Because hearts cry too into focus is
What happens when you come into view
—And it's a healing thing for me, I hope for you too.

# XXII

I don't know much about here
But in New York
The streets have a way of teaching you the hard way
What you refused to learn easily at home

# XXIII

She told the doctor she was dying
He told her she's lying
The next day she dropped to the floor
—On her knees she was thanking the Lord for life.

# XXIV

Her nipples
Gave me cause to re-evaluate my position
Because I could see the truth.

# XXV

Images of pictures I took
Collage in my head, like a rainbow
—My memory, my thoughts of you
Were complete.

# XXVI

Hiding behind the door
Kept away the shame
That caused more, more pain
And it is from that pain
Today's gain was made.

# And My Lover Calls

It's Friday night,
I'm home alone again
And again the nighttime makes the boredom rise.
As time goes by, my lover calls.
I balance the urges beneath my feet.

And my lover calls with pretense of filling needs.
Ecstasy and pain; I call you by your name.
I pause
To maintain,
To stay away from this refrain.

You seduce me with mental images
Of great orgasms I'd gladly crawl for
On all fours-at one time.
Not even to ask what, when, why, or how,
—And sorrow be awaiting at the end.
—Just not today,
My lover calls this time with illusions,
With the rationalizations of
What defines creativity to an artist.
I know your lies too well.
Send in the clowns to rid the frowns
Or we'll toast for breakfast
With Little Debbie's, shame, blame and regret
I know too well your lies

Alone in the dark,
I stand in my room by the window


My God stands beside me.
No need to twist fancy words into fancy concepts
For superficial thrills
As long as I know who you really are (my lover)
Ecstasy and pain; I call you by your name.

# In This Face

In this face
That buries my pain that buries my fears relieved
That bless my thoughts into Precious time—
With grace to say;
To those faces that are blind,
You can see too.
If you first believe the truth.

In this face
That holds my tears—
To behold and embrace God's peace
To share among us all
That bless my thoughts into precious time—
With grace to say;
To those faces that are blind,
You can see too.
If you first believe
The simple truth—that you can.
Amen.

# Lucky's Great Adventure

Snow cracked tree limbs
And branches barricade the front yard rough neck
Miniature jungle adventure in the snow
For little Lucky.

# XXVII

She wrote a self psycho analytical diary of poetry
She said could be a resolution of inner conflict
She said the therapeutic value of honesty
Could be priceless.

# Slam I

You are so busy manipulating the pennies,
You're missing the dollars
The real treasure- friendship.

# Christmases Hooked "S"

In poise of respect, with the grace to protect,
Stern of dexterity communicates sincerity
—Ease steady the speed on these leads…
The come, the go to cling noise and bow
The word genuflect makes your lips move now.
Like they do to goo-goo, gaga on site of a special baby-born.

Dupe, stoop, page, and nephew thump-a-bump some
Scatters tatter, but can Rumple-still-skin
A deer without stopping to stutter?
Then hurray for you put an "H"
On your chest but can you handle hot peas
And butter without stopping
Cause Christmases hooked "S" is something else.

The Magi came from far lands
Bearing gifts in acknowledgement to the promise kept
—Of hope for a better tomorrow
A king the acme of consideration
(discipline and manners) has come into the world
To save us by his compassion.
They followed the brilliance of a star as their only route

Root and route often said the same way travel far apart
Like some routes start at the beginning other routes we follow
Sometimes semantics dictates potato, tomato-tomato
Spices, Isis, Plato and I would also
Have gone to see this special baby too.

*"If you haven't guessed by now*
*or maybe out- to- lunch with Tight Lipped and Tongue*
*Loosen the two of them- let*
*the sound free to communicate world peace eloquently.*
*—We're celebrating the birth of hope*
*for all mankind in this one special baby- born."*

Lopez winds a spinning top
At Winthrop perfectly without stopping
Reggie likes tricycles:
Try you, Try he, She, It and I
Try we are going past the tricycle shop—
With a gift for you
Three kids and I cause
Christmases hooked"S"
From any lipped side to the other
Is really something else.
Merry Christmas—to you
Merry Christmas to you—smiling
Merry Christmas, Merry Christmas
Merry Christmas to you too.

# Dark In Question

Whether day or night was unknown to me at the time,
But what I did know were the flames inside the woodstove,
Along with a controlling darkness, intrigued me…
Because it was cold and dark outside,
The house was cold and dark inside so we gathered for warmth.
We gathered for clarity as our minds wondered the possibilities
Of worldwide economic relapse.
Our minds wondered to question:
Would time become a witness
As to the true civility of our great nation and
How would this generation survive a great depression?
After a long while, we laughed, amused with ourselves
Engaging our minds to such wonders.
—Were we drinking yard grass already
Calling it grass straw tea too soon?

# Manners

A child is wise when they are aware to consider
Self and others

A child is wise who's well balanced thoughts conclude,
To the understanding- all life is special.

A child is wise when their discipline
Is not governed by fear of punishment.
But by the reflection of what is good in their parents.

Kids are going to be kids but
A wise child has curiosities that demand explanation
For confirming or verification-
This child maybe a talker but eventually learns to listen.
With application of vision-
They also learn the value of good grooming early.

A wise child is so adult, their only struggle is for humility
(They'll find it quicker in charity of service
under God our heavenly Father)

A wise child loves his parents, cherishes them dearly
And first shows that love by continued actions of obedience
In and out of their presence-
It is that which separates them far from the others.

The child who's state of mind complies with a persistent
Hunger and thirst for wanting to know and do better,
I believe to be by far, the wisest of them all.
By their example, they invite and inspire us all
To strive and continue to grow
Strive and continue to grow.

# Naked on the Roam

She was a stranger then
When she told me
Her father played a game with her
And the mayonnaise jar
Whenever they were alone in the home
The game had a name
He called it Naked on the Roam

She said the house became like a jungle
As she looked for a place to hide
That Dad only wore a towel round his waist
Whenever he came hunting to find

Once he found her
He always said your lucky
Only big girls can play this game
As he wiped the sweat and tears
From her tensed little body, face, and eyes...
Once he found her
She was to ready herself for her big surprise.
Five and a half Gerber jars long and one Gerber jar wide.

By the age of nine
She said the mayonnaise jar was no longer required
No longer part of the game
Although there was still pain it was somehow not the same
Now having money in her pocket made
A difference

Her mother retired too that year
Which meant they would no longer be alone in the home
And so he took her to hotel rooms
Where she would get her allowance
Twenty-Five dollars a week
For playing his little game
The game he called Naked on the Roam.

And yet it was with a joyful tone
She said to me—she loves her Dad
Who manipulated fun into pain,
A frightened daughters' love into a mayonnaise jar,
—Too scared to pray
Gave her a permanent twitch and switch
To her walk to replace the childhood he took—
And the education he stole away.

And yet it was with a joyful tone
She said to me
She was grateful to her Dad
For showing her this way
To have fun in hotels and get paid
She said made school a real waste of her time
And that's all she would ever say

What is this poem about?
I thought if I could label or title it now
I could at least control its outcome somehow

At first I thought
A victims love for her predator Dad
Or
Stockholm syndrome
Or
A father's misplaced love for his child
Or
Forgiveness home runs from left field?
Or
Family secrets of hide go seek
Or
Effects of an absentee mom
Or
What is this poem really about
Is it about me or you or who or what
Could it be about sons whose stories stay secret
About sons
Who can't unload their burdens
Through casual conversation
Could it be about sons
That have been hurt
By sons that have been hurt
Maybe even by sons that have been hurt
Could it be about those sons
Who just by their nature break the cycle
And want us to know—need for us to know
Hurt people don't have to hurt
Because the world is a better place
Hurt people don't have to hurt

# Without Words

Sinner that I was—that I am
Oh Lord
Without words you heard me
Without delay you were there for me in dawn's approaching
I remember that morning
It was then and there i first called you boss too.

In the mirror looking
At someone else staring back at me...
In grips of fear—panics unspoken tear.

You came in dawn's approaching
—That twist into fusion
—That combust with composure,
Tranquil parade marching pageantry forward,
A majestic sky.

Without words
This beauty that was correspondent to me and
Communication made clear,
To the gravity full I was to become—whole
Relieved to see
Who was once more me, looking back, in the mirror at me

And without direction
You came without boundaries
Sinner that I was—that I am
Without words you heard me
And yeah—way!

**Biographical note from the author:**

"With all the mistakes I've made so far in life,
I won't embarrass the institutions I've attended.
Although school is so very important,
Education fundamental to any civilized society,
Life has a way of teaching what's not
Learned in school.
I think those lessons and experiences
Are so much more interesting
What is really important
Is how we apply what is learned"

*Phillip Regman,*
*Native New Yorker*
*now resides in California*

**Painting entitled "Crash"**
**By Mary Ann Kikerpill**

Mary Ann Kikerpill is an Outsider artist. She lives at her very secluded Holy Mountain Dream Ranch at the foot of Mt. Shasta in Northern California. Her passion is to paint what she is feeling on the canvas in the simplest way that she can. Her artwork represents her life journey as a first generation American woman.

**Painting entitled "Ella and Byrd"**
**By Armando Alleyne**

Armando Alleyne has been painting his Afro-Expressionistic style over the last decade. Currently he focuses on Jazz musicians as the theme. He mostly paints in acrylic with some collage.

9 781897 475652